GETTING THE JOB DONE

OIL RIG WORKERS

Jill Sherman

PowerKiDS press

New York

Published in 2020 by The Rosen Publishing Group, Inc.
29 East 21st Street, New York, NY 10010

First Edition

Editor: Greg Roza
Book Design: Reann Nye

Photo Credits: Cover, p. 18 brazzo/iStock Unreleased/Getty Images; p. 5 REDPIXEL.PL/Shutterstock.com; p. 7 hiroshi teshigawara/Shutterstock.com; p. 8 Lukasz Z/Shutterstock.com; p. 9 mikeuk/E+/Getty Images; p. 11 Rumo/ Shutterstock.com; p. 12 sirtravelalot/Shutterstock.com; p. 13 HHakim/E+/Getty Images; p. 15 Eddytb Foto/Shutterstock.com; p. 16 Polina Petrenko/Shutterstock. com; p. 17 AzmanMD/Shutterstock.com; p. 19 curraheeshutter/Shutterstock.com; p. 21 think4photop/Shutterstock.com; p. 22 noomcpk/Shutterstock.com.

Cataloging-in-Publication Data

Names: Sherman, Jill.
Title: Oil rig workers / Jill Sherman.
Description: New York : PowerKids Press, 2020. | Series: Getting the job done | Includes glossary and index.
Identifiers: ISBN 9781725300088 (pbk.) | ISBN 9781725300101 (library bound) | ISBN 9781725300095 (6pack)
Subjects: LCSH: Oil well drilling–Juvenile literature. | Oil well drilling rigs–Juvenile literature. | Offshore oil industry–Accidents–Juvenile literature.
Classification: LCC TN871.2 S54 2020 | DDC 622.3382'023–dc23

Manufactured in the United States of America

CPSIA Compliance Information: Batch #CSPK19. For Further Information contact Rosen Publishing, New York, New York at 1-800-237-9932.

CONTENTS

OIL IN OUR LIVES

Oil heats our homes. It powers our cars. It is used to create electricity. It is used to make plastic products. Oil touches our lives in many ways. The United States uses more oil than any other country. But that oil has to come from somewhere. It must be **extracted** from the earth. That's what oil rig workers do!

This is tough work. But oil rig workers play an important role in helping America get the oil it needs. Do you have what it takes to tackle the different kinds of jobs that oil rig workers do? Let's find out!

Oil is used to create gasoline, which powers cars, trucks, and other vehicles. >

5

WHERE DOES OIL COME FROM?

Petroleum is a **natural resource**. It is a black liquid found in the earth. It is considered a fossil fuel. This means that it was formed from the remains of plants and animals that lived millions of years ago. Over time, the remains were covered by mud and dirt. Heat and pressure turned the remains into coal, oil, and natural gas.

Scientists locate different fossil fuels under the earth's surface. Coal is mined from the earth while natural gas is pumped out. Oil is most commonly extracted as a thin, brown or black liquid. It is then processed so that it can be used to make gasoline and other items.

The first U.S. oil company dates back to 1859. >

STRIKING OIL

Oil is a very valuable resource. Companies will spend a lot of money to find and drill for oil. It is the job of oil rig workers to extract oil from deep under the earth's surface.

Fascinating Career Facts

There are about 200 people on an oil rig at any time. During their off hours, oil rig workers can spend time at the gym, watching movies, playing games, and catching up with loved ones back home.

Oil rig workers sleep in small cabins while they are on a job.

There are two types of oil drilling: onshore and offshore. Onshore oil drilling is when the oil rig is on land. The rig is in water for offshore drilling. Oil rig workers must travel to wherever the oil is. Most workers live on-site. They spend weeks away from their families and friends. The oil site becomes like a small town. There are buildings where the workers live, eat, and relax.

LIFE ON THE RIG

The job on an oil rig is to extract oil. But it can be very difficult work. That oil may be buried thousands of meters deep. The oil rig crew works together to get the job done.

Most who are new to the job start as **roustabouts**. They carry equipment and clean up. They watch and learn from the more experienced workers.

Roughnecks have a more demanding job. They are in charge of the drill. They use heavy tools to connect new sections of pipe. They climb the rig to make repairs. They also keep the equipment working.

Roughnecks keep the drill running all day and all night.

Drillers oversee the drill operation. They tell roughnecks when to change out equipment. They watch the flow of drill fluid. This is also called "mud." The fluid keeps the drill cool while it runs. It also helps carry the dirt and rock out of the hole so the drill can go deeper.

In addition, there are other workers with **specialized** skills. There are **welders**, electricians, crane operators, and more.

Fascinating Career Facts

Not all jobs on an oil rig are about oil. Since the rig runs like a miniature town, it also employs doctors, cooks, cleaners, and others.

Welders put together oil pipelines. They may also make repairs to the rig. Welders on offshore rigs may have special training in underwater welding.

An oil rig operates 24 hours a day. Drilling is done in 12-hour shifts. Riggers work in all kinds of weather. By the end of the day most workers are covered in grease. This creates one tough work day.

13

A DANGEROUS JOB

Working on an oil rig is a dangerous job. Workers have to pay attention to safety. The job requires they wear hard hats and steel-toed boots. The machines are very loud. Workers often wear earplugs to protect their hearing.

But the biggest risk on an oil rig is fire. Workers are around heavy machinery and materials that could explode all day. One spark could **ignite** a huge fire. Big **explosions** are rare but they do happen. Workers complete safety training so they know what to do if **disaster** strikes. Safety first is the best policy for any job on a rig!

Fascinating Career Facts

Working on an oil rig is one of the most dangerous jobs in the United States. About 108 people die working on oil rigs every year.

14

All activities are monitored on an oil rig.
In the event of an emergency, workers
will be able to react quickly.

TRAINING AND EDUCATION

If you are interested in becoming an oil rig worker, you must have a high school diploma. Often, this is enough to get started as a roustabout. Only a few jobs on the rig require a college education.

Oil rig workers perform a training exercise on how to close a well in case of an emergency.

Certificates and on-the-job training are more important for oil rig workers. Those working offshore will have to complete more safety training. All offshore workers must complete a Basic Offshore Safety **Induction** and Emergency Training (BOSIET) program. The class takes three days. It teaches them safety rules, first aid, how to handle **hazardous** materials, and emergency response. Helicopter Underwater Emergency Training (HUET) may also be required.

17

OIL RIGGER INCOME

The salary for an oil rig worker depends on what the job is. Roustabout is the most common job on an oil rig. In the United States, a roustabout can expect to earn about $37,000 per year according to the U.S. Bureau of Labor Statistics. Roughnecks will earn about $46,000. Supervisors earn more. A drilling supervisor may earn about $80,000 per year.

Fascinating Career Facts

Most oil rig workers are men but women do the job as well. About 27 percent of oil rig workers are women. It's a job for everyone!

Working on an oil rig is a job that can have its rewards. The longer someone works there, the better chance they have for a better job. This will come with better pay, too.

Over time, the more experience and the more certificates you get will help you earn even more. Roustabouts may earn as much as $59,000 per year. Roughnecks can earn up to $64,000 per year.

A GROWING INDUSTRY

The U.S. Bureau of Labor Statistics says the future for oil rig workers looks bright. Over the next 10 years, 12,400 new jobs are expected to be created. That means the industry will grow by 25 percent. That's much faster than the average job.

The need for oil is always present in the way we live. It helps heat our homes, run our cars, and create electricity. We will continue to rely on oil for our energy needs. As long as there are oil deposits to be mined in America or across the world, oil rig workers will have jobs.

Fascinating Career Facts

Oil rigs are massive structures that reach down to the sea floor. Some are 4,000 feet (1,219 m) tall. That's taller than the world's biggest skyscrapers.

Oil rig workers work as a team to decide the best way to drill and complete the job. The teams help keep each other safe, too.

UP TO THE CHALLENGE?

Working on an oil rig is a great opportunity that allows someone to enter the career quickly. Many companies are hiring workers for positions on oil rigs.

But the job is hard work. Workers must be strong and physically fit. Rigs operate 24 hours a day. Rig workers must always be ready to respond in case of an emergency. Workers must also be able to work as part of a team. They will be away from their families for long periods of time so they will have to rely on team members for help on and off the rig.

GLOSSARY

certificate: A document that proves someone completed specialized training.

disaster: A sudden event that causes damage and loss.

explosion: A sudden bursting out of heat and fire.

extract: To pull something out of something else.

hazardous: Involving or exposing one to loss or harm.

ignite: To catch fire or cause fire.

induction: The act of causing or bringing about something.

natural resource: Something from nature that humans find useful.

petroleum: Unrefined oil.

roughneck: A skilled laborer on an oil rig.

roustabout: An unskilled laborer on an oil rig.

specialize: To focus one's attention or skill on a certain subject.

welder: A worker who joins pieces of metal together using heat.

23

INDEX

WEBSITES

Due to the changing nature of Internet links, PowerKids Press has developed an online list of websites related to the subject of this book. This site is updated regularly. Please use this link to access the list: www.powerkidslinks.com/GTJD/oilrig